Ancient Mosaics

Other titles in this series:

Cassell's Introducing Archaeology Series

Ancient Mosaics

MICHAEL AVI-YONAH

Cassell · London

CASSELL & COMPANY LTD
35 Red Lion Square, London WC1R 4SG
Sydney, Auckland
Toronto, Johannesburg

Designed by Ofra Kamar
Assistant designer Felix Graber

First published in Great Britain 1975

I.S.B.N. 0 304 29335 0

Printed by Peli Printing Works, Ltd., Givataim.

PRINTED IN ISRAEL

F. 173

CONTENTS

FROM MUSE TO MOSAIC

The Muses — the nine companions of Apollo — were Greek deities of poetry, literature, music and dance, and later also of astronomy, philosophy and various intellectual pursuits. Although no particular Muse was associated with mosaic art, it is from their name, paradoxically, that the word "mosaic" was originally derived. In the late Latin of the 4th century AD the term for this art form was *pictum de musio* or *opus musivum*. In classical Latin, mosaic art was also called *opus tessellatum*, from the word *tessella*, meaning a small square cube. The Greeks kept the name *psephosis*, from the word *psephos*, meaning pebble — the earliest mosaics were made from this material.

The very dawn of humanity saw the start of mosaic art: it began in the Mesolithic or Middle Stone Age (10,000–7500 BC). Inventive cavemen with artistic talent initiated the art of mosaics by inserting pieces of coloured material into the hollowed-out surfaces of various objects. Bone knife handles and other similar tools are the earliest forms of their work.

Left: Hellenistic mosaic from Pompeii.

1. *The First Mosaics*

The famous Standard of Ur in Mesopotamia shows early mosaic work — from about 2600 BC. Blue *lapis lazuli* and red limestones were used to fashion pictures on a bitumen base. This same technique is found again at Erech (Warka) in Mesopotamia, where small cone-shaped pieces of clay with painted surfaces were inserted in mud plaster to form designs on walls and columns.

Further examples of early mosaic art have been found in Egypt. A wellknown example is the ivories of Samaria from the Ivory House of King Ahab of Israel (9th century BC), which are also decorated with inlaid work. Incisions were cut into the ivory plaques and were then filled with small pieces of coloured stone.

Until recently there was a historical gap in our knowledge of mosaic art, since little was known about the progress of the mosaic tradition between the period of the ancient Greeks and the earliest mosaics found in Greece itself. Recently, however, the excavations carried out at Gordium revealed the information required to fill this lacuna. Gordium, in Asia Minor, where the famous Gordian knot was cut by Alexander the Great, was the capital of Phrygia in the 8th century BC. The mosaic pavements found at this site were made of decorated pebbles, which were then arranged in various geometrical designs. The Gordium mosaics of the 8th, 7th, and 6th centuries BC are very significant, because they furnish the missing link in time and space between the earlier Oriental mosaics and the Greek mosaic art which began to flourish in the 4th century BC.

I GREEK AND HELLENISTIC MOSAICS

1. *Early Greek Mosaics*

The best preserved early Greek mosaics have been found at Olynthus, a city in the Chalcidic peninsula which was destroyed by Philip II of Macedonia (Alexander's father) in 348 BC. This act of destruction has served archaeologists well, since it established that all finds on the site must be dated to earlier than 348 BC.

The Olynthus mosaics are typical of the early stages of fourth-century Greek mosaics. One can see at a glance that the style of mosaics produced at that time was derived from vase paintings rather than wall paintings. They imitate the red-figured Attic vases, on which human figures in the reddish clay background colour stand out against the black glaze used on the vessels. Similarly, the Olynthus mosaics have a black pebble background, and the figures and decorations appear in pebbles of a bright reddish, white, green, or blue colour.

The representations on the mosaics are taken mainly from the world of Greek mythology. In some cases, pavements reproduce symbols which were thought to bring luck or ward off evil — stars, for example. In the House of the Mosaic of the Nereids (Nereus, "the old man of the sea", had 50 daughters called the Nereids) we find a procession of sea goddesses carrying the arms of Achilles as they ride over the sea on dolphins and hippocamps (seahorses).

In yet another Olynthus mosaic, the mythical hero Bellerophon appears on his famous winged horse, Pegasus. Bellerophon, who killed the lion-headed, serpent-tailed monster called Chimera, is dressed as a Corinthian cavalier. He is shown riding above the monster while attacking it with his spear.

Other fourth-century mosaics were found at the Temple of Zeus at Olynthus; these depict dolphins, Tritons and Cupids in frames of flowing leaf design. These works are of the same style as the mosaics from Motya in Sicily, and all of them are made of pebbles and were used as floors in

Bellerophon, 4th century Olynthus mosaic

A deer hunt mosaic from Pella

houses. Regrettably, no wall mosaics from this period have survived.

2. *The Pella Mosaics*

From the early Greek mosaics we move on to the fully developed Hellenistic mosaics, through an intermediate stage represented by the works discovered at Pella. From this city, the capital of the Macedonian kingdom, Alexander the Great launched his victorious campaigns against Persia. Although Pella remained a capital city until 167 BC, all the mosaics found there date from the late 4th or early 3rd century BC. As in earlier Greek products, all these mosaics are made of pebbles, although they differ from the earlier colour schemes of black and red with the addition of other colours.

The Pella mosaics are even closer in style to Greek painting than those found at Olynthus. The finest of these objects represent the following scenes: the Rape of Helena by Theseus the Athenian; a fight between Greeks and Amazons; and a deer hunt. Each is enclosed in a wide border decorated with images of animals and palmettes.

In the Rape of Helena mosaic, the tradition of older vase painting is still very much in evidence. The names of the characters are written above the images. In all other aspects, however, the work represents the finest tradition of classical art at its best. The four horses pulling Theseus' chariot are drawn with masterly oblique perspective. The clothing as well as the movements of Helena and Dione are most carefully and exactly depicted.

The deer-hunt mosaic represents two hunters whose cloaks are waving wildly in the wind. One of them is seizing a deer by its antlers with one hand while swinging his sword with the other. The hunter's hat, the *petasos,* floats in the air behind him. The second hunter is preparing to reach out with a battle-axe to finish the job. A hound is holding the deer from the other side.

The mosaic is distinguished by two features. First, it is the earliest mosaic known to us which was signed by the artist, in this case a man named Gnosis.

Secondly, there is a most elaborate border of lilies and acanthus which winds around the central field of the scene. The twistings and curvings are done in a three-dimensional manner with a special quality of movement, very unusual in early mosaic art.

Aside from these fine mosaics, the Pella works include a pavement of great historical interest. It represents a hunting scene, in which a lion is placing a paw on the foot of one of the hunters. The hunter, whose face expresses pain, and even fear, is wearing a Macedonian hat.

Behind the lion another hunter, carrying the slightly curved Macedonian sword, is reaching out with a mighty stroke to kill the animal. In this mosaic the limbs of the figures are indicated as three-dimensional by their shading. Also, a bent leg, in profile, is shown in the correct anatomical position and an extended leg is seen from the front; all of which give depth to the scene. This representation has been explained as the story of Alexander's rescue during a hunt by his companion Cassander. Obviously, this representation could not have been made during Alexander's lifetime or those of his immediate successors. But later, when Cassander became ruler of Macedonia, he boasted of the exploit, which could explain the historical reference to the event. Cassander, in fact, ordered this same scene to be executed in bronze at the city of Delphi.

In all the Pella mosaics we notice an interesting technical detail that has not been found in many others — thin strips of lead were used to mark the body contours and internal features of the human beings.

A hunting scene from Pella

3. *Hellenistic Mosaics*

It is in the Hellenistic period, between the years 323 and 30 BC, that the first literary reference to the existence and use of mosaics appears. It seems that a luxury sea-going vessel was built by Hieron, tyrant of Syracuse, and presented by him to Ptolemy II, King of Egypt, who lived in the first half of the 3rd century BC. In a description of the ship, we read that one of the banqueting rooms was laid out with a *lithostratos* (which means that the floor was inlaid with stones) forming designs representing scenes from one of Homer's epics. An additional literary reference has been preserved in Pliny's *Natural History*. In the thirty-sixth volume, Pliny refers to the use of stone in mosaics:

> "The Greeks were the first to decorate floors with mosaic. The most celebrated worker in mosaic is Sosus who laid the floors of a house at Pergamun, known as the 'unswept house' because he represented, in small bits of many-coloured mosaic, the scraps from the table and everything that is usually swept away as if they had been left lying on the floor. Among these mosaics is a marvellous dove drinking and casting the shadow of its head on the water. Other doves are preening their feathers in the sun on the lip of the goblet."

By chance, a copy of each of these famous mosaics has been preserved. A pavement found at Rome depicts various remains of a meal such as the wishbone of a chicken, the remains of crabs, the backbone of a fish, and nutshells. All these objects are shown casting their shadows on the floor, which has obviously been left unswept. The second mosaic described by Pliny has also been preserved in a late copy from the villa of the Emperor Hadrian (2nd century AD). It depicts three doves — one of them leaning over to drink, another preening — perched on the rim of a vase full of water.

Also found at Pergamum were the earliest examples of mosaics imitating carpets covering the floor. The fringe of the carpets is reproduced in the form of a line of battlements or knots with fringes.

During the Hellenistic period, a second centre of Greek mosaic art flourished on the island of Delos. From the 2nd century onwards, an important commercial area developed there, and trade relations were carried on from Italy to the Orient. Various mosaic representations were found in the houses at Delos, showing scenes which include Dionysus on his panther and Cupids riding on dolphins. Because Delos was destroyed by pirates in 69 BC, and has remained in ruins ever since, these mosaics are more or less exactly dated.

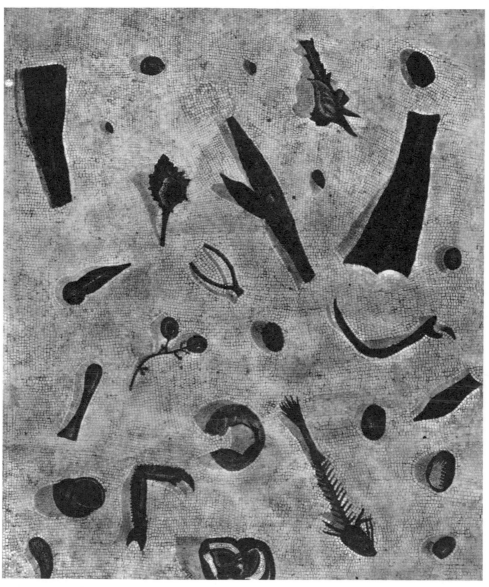

The "Unswept" floor

The Palestrina mosaic

The third centre of mosaic art was at Alexandria, the Hellenistic capital of the kingdom of Egypt. Because of its unique position, this Greek city was always described as standing "near" or "off" Egypt — it was never described as part of the country whose capital it was.

Unfortunately, very few remains from the Alexandria of the Hellenistic and Roman periods have survived. But echoes of Egyptian and Greco-Egyptian mosaic art have been preserved by means of various copies which were dispersed throughout the Roman Empire.

A Nilotic scene, Pompeii

Most of these represented life in the Nile Valley. Several of the exotic temples built at that time still stand today. These buildings, executed in the native Egyptian style, aroused the admiration and wonder of the Greeks and Romans. In antiquity, Egypt held the same position as China in the 18th century — it was a remote country full of wonderful objects whose interesting style was well worth imitating.

One of the earliest of these Egyptian-

Pompeii mosaic showing actor's mask, fruit and floral decoration

style mosaics (called Nilotic, because of the River Nile) was found at Palestrina near Rome. The mosaic, dated to about 80 BC, shows a view of the whole Nile Valley, starting with the Greek villas and ships near Alexandria and ending in the Sudan. In the section nearest the observer, boats are arriving and a feast is being held under a tent. Behind this scene, the Nile Valley is shown at the time of its annual flood. Boats are travelling up and down the river, and

A stage rehearsal, Pompeii

straw-roofed huts are all over the area.
A sanctuary for ibises, the sacred birds
of the Egyptians, is flanked on one side
by the remains of an Egyptian temple
which is depicted complete with its
pylons (gateway structures) and colossal
statues near the gates. On the other side,
there is a ruin, and beyond it a procession is entering the temple of Isis, which
is built in the Greek style. Behind this
civilized part of the Nile Valley, the
wilderness of the Sudan is shown full of
Africans fighting wild animals. This
scene continues until images of dragons
and all kinds of mythical beings appear
at the top of the picture — these
mythical creatures were meant to represent the unknown interior of Africa.
Similar Nilotic scenes have been found
throughout the ancient Roman Empire,
including Palestine.

One section of a mosaic preserved at
Alexandria shows the city as a woman
with wide-open eyes; she is being

crowned by a galley. This is an allusion to the port of Alexandria, the principal source of the city's wealth. The mosaic is signed by the artist Sophilus.

Other remnants or copies of Hellenistic mosaics have been found at Pompeii, one of the cities near Naples which was covered by the eruption of Vesuvius in AD 79. Pompeii was originally a Greek town, and in it are preserved many examples of Hellenistic art.

One remarkable feature of Hellenistic life was the great importance of the theatre. In fact, Greek theatrical art was a most valuable means for spreading Greek culture in both the East and the West. It is no wonder, then, that many mosaics found at Pompeii represent theatrical scenes. In the famous "Rehearsal", we see a producer distributing masks to a group of actors as they put on their costumes. Two other mosaics with similar themes have been found at Pompeii, both signed by the artist

Roving street musicians, Dioscorides mosaic

The battle between Alexander the Great and Darius III

Detail of Alexander from battle scene mosaic

Dioscorides of Samos. We are not sure, however, that these Pompeiian mosaics, now in the Naples Museum, are actually the work of this artist: it is possible that someone copied them and copied the signature as well.

One of the mosaics shows the scene of a lovesick maiden consulting a hideous old hag who is pretending to foretell the future from a vase. The girl is accompanied by a friend. At the edge of the picture we see the fortune-teller's slave.

The second "Dioscorides" mosaic shows a troupe of roving street musicians. Three of them — two men and a woman — are wearing masks. One is playing a drum, another is dancing and playing the castanets, and the woman is playing a flute. An unmasked and sad-faced street child standing behind the woman represents the reality behind the smiling masks of the actors. These mosaics, especially that of the street musicians, are of a very high technical standard. The exact colours of a painting are reproduced, and the shadows cast by the figures are projected on the wall behind them with masterly skill.

The only existing example of the rare Greek historical painting style was also found at Pompeii. The painting has been translated into a mosaic representing the battle between Alexander and Darius III, King of Persia. It shows a face-to-face encounter between the two men, which probably occurred at the Battle of Issus in 333 BC. In this work, the artist has reduced an earth-shaking conflict to its simplest dimensions. The actual meeting of the two leaders shows the significance of a major historical development at one

Detail of Darius from battle scene mosaic

quick glance. On the left side of the picture, we see Alexander charging forward at the head of his cavalry. In the centre of the scene to the right, Darius is shown in his chariot, in great danger of being captured. A Persian nobleman has thrown himself between the king and the enemy to save his royal master. He pays dearly, however, for his courage. A missile strikes his horse and he himself is pierced by Alexander's lance. Another Persian nobleman has descended from his horse to assist the first, but he is too late. The sacrifice of the brave Persian, however, has not been in vain, for he has gained a few extra moments for his king. The charioteer uses them to gallop away as fast as possible, and we see him wielding his whip alongside the king. In the meantime, the Persian cavalry is advancing into the gap between Alexander and Darius. More help is coming from the right in reply to urgent hand signals. Darius himself is represented in exact accordance with literary descriptions of Persian kings; with his high tiara and necklace, he is truly a royal figure. Although he is in imminent danger of being captured, Darius does not appear to be thinking of his own peril. He is stretching out

his hand to try to help the loyal man who sacrificed himself to save his king. This act of royal humanity throws a glorious light on the defeated ruler. The victorious Alexander, on the other hand, expresses the iron will of the Macedonian conqueror. His face bears a concentrated expression, his eyes are wide open and he presses forward with an irresistible urge. The artist used very few colours in this painting and very little landscape as well, except for a barren, chopped-off tree. A row of lances forms the background, reminding us of the famous Surrender of Breda by Velázquez.

There is one technical feature common to these Hellenistic mosaics and to the Roman ones which followed them. The pictures themselves were known technically as *emblema*. They were prepared in workshops and then brought to the location where the floor was to be laid. There they were set in a wide border or even a whole field of floral or geometric design. The battle scene described above was placed in this manner. Often, the geometric designs were given the shape of panels inset in the ceiling, producing the illusion of a reflection on the floor.

II PAVEMENTS OF THE ROMAN EMPIRE

In the Roman Imperial period (from the 1st to the 3rd centuries AD), the art of mosaic production spread throughout the whole empire. Of course, this did not happen all at once, in fact a certain chronological and stylistic development can be observed. The art form began to spread from Italy, in the heart of the empire, and probably also from the great Hellenistic centres of Antioch in Syria and Alexandria in Egypt. Gradually, mosaic art reached into the farthest corners of the empire, such as Africa, Gaul, Germany, and Britain.

1. Ostia

The black and white style of mosaics can be seen best at Ostia, the ancient port of Rome, now a seaside resort. Although Ostia became Rome's harbour in the 1st century AD, its development dates mainly from Trajan, Hadrian, and the Antonine emperors who followed them in the 2nd century. The mosaics of Ostia show that the artists of that period gave up the attempt to reproduce pictures with perspective and the use of colouring and shading. Instead, they preferred designs done in black on a white background, with inner divisions of the pictures represented by white lines. The beginnings of this style can be noticed in works from Pompeii which date to before AD 79. The full stylistic development, however, was achieved in Rome and Ostia in the 2nd century.

Many of the Ostia mosaics were found in baths, and so there is a preponderance of maritime scenes. In one of these, Poseidon, god of the seas (known as Neptune to the Romans), is represented on his chariot drawn by four horses with fish-tails. He is surrounded by a floating procession of various animals or mythical creatures, such as centaurs. There is also a whole series of mosaics in which are depicted a sea-bull, a sea-goat, a sea-donkey, and similar animals.

Another famous mosaic from Ostia shows the various types of carriages used by the Romans. Methods of land and sea transport are shown, as well as four giants supporting a square-shaped city, the plan of a Roman colony. Because Ostia always harboured ships, corporations of merchants from all parts of the empire lived in the city. One of the most famous Ostia mosaics depicts the many harbours from which boats came to Ostia, and also shows the men working on the ships in these foreign ports. These mosaics give us an all-round picture of the activity in the harbour of Rome at that time.

2. *Africa*

From Italy, mosaic art spread to Africa. Thousands of mosaics have been found in the Roman provinces of Mauretania, Numidia, and Africa itself (which is today Tunis). They decorate the floors of baths, public buildings, villas, and temples. All aspects of ancient life were illustrated — mythology, sporting competitions, arts and crafts, and especially rural life. These pictures

Sea donkey, mosaic from Ostia

are very valuable in that they help us understand the various technical aspects of agriculture of that period. On the whole, the African mosaics do not follow the black and white traditions of second-century Italy. They are colourful and vivid, and sometimes their subjects are cruel — most indicative of life in the Berber provinces under the burning sun of Africa.

A mosaic of this type was found in a villa at Zliten, in what is now Libya. It shows the fullest representation ever found of gladiatorial combat and the execution of prisoners of war by wild beasts. Every detail of these games is depicted. We see the band which played before the fights; the actual fights between the gladiators; the exposure of people, bound to moveable stakes, to wild animals; and so on.

The mosaics discovered in Africa help

Gladiatorial combat from a villa at Zliten

us follow the whole development of Roman art. Beginning with the impressionism of the Flavian period, they show the transition to the realism of the Antonines and to the romantic and expressive character of art in the time of Septimus Severus and his successors. Throughout these periods, mosaic artists divided floors into geometric panels in order to represent a series of subjects. They liked to use subjects which would represent unity and at the same time allow for many subdivisions, such as the Twelve Months or the Twelve Labours of Hercules.

3. *Antioch*

Many examples of mosaic art have also been found at Antioch, the capital of Roman Syria. Pavements were excavated and carefully dated from the period of Trajan (early 2nd century AD) to the beginning of the Byzantine era. In general, mosaic art in Antioch developed just as it did in the rest of the Roman empire. The pictures are mainly of the *emblema* variety—enclosed scenes of a certain subject placed within a wide border which was not connected to the theme of the picture. Gradually, however, the artists began to enlarge the area of the scene until it came to cover almost the whole surface of the pavement.

The subjects of the pictures found at Antioch are mainly mythological. Most of them deal with the worship of Dionysus, the Greek god of wine. Many were arranged in the centre of banqueting rooms, where they could be viewed with ease from the couches on which the Romans reclined to dine. Three of these pavements represent the competition between Hercules and Dionysus, in which the great hero is defeated by the god of wine — a subject suitable for the banquet hall when the company competed to see who could drink the most wine.

Other mosaics represent many aspects of Greek mythology. There was a special preference for scenes which had been the subject of classical Greek drama. These combined mythology and theatrical life, two of the main sources of inspiration for mosaic pavements all over the Roman empire. Additional pavements show mystical religious ceremonies, such as the worship of Isis, the Egyptian goddess whose worship spread through the whole Roman empire.

In the 3rd and early 4th centuries, the Roman empire was beset by a period of great internal conflict. There was a general crisis which was economic and political at the same time, and in the end also religious. During that entire period, mosaics tended to represent either philosophical conceptions such as

A drinking contest from Antioch

Time in relation to man's life, or the Seasons and other calendar subjects. They served to remind the populace that although time was fleeting, everything would return to its rightful place each year. The annual change of the Seasons gave hope that the difficult winter would pass and that the good times of spring and summer would return. The people of that period strove desperately for a sense of social security and for the fulfilment of the simple demands of a peaceful life. The mosaics of this era, therefore, represented personifications of man's ambitions: security, absence of preoccupation, quietness, or even eating one's fill. (The state of satiety — *tryphé* in Greek — was one of the most commonly represented personifications of the time.) Other representations include generosity *(megalopsychia)*, the distribution of the good things in life, foundation *(ktisis)* — in honour of the founder of houses, power *(dynamis)* and so on. These embodiments serve to indicate what the people of that time were lacking most.

One particular fourth-century mosaic from Antioch is typical of this period of crisis. In this mosaic, *chresis* (usefulness) presents gifts on a tablet to *ktisis* (the personified foundation of Antioch). The gold, jewellery, and sparkling diamonds are most skilfully executed with mosaic cubes.

There are also a number of mosaics at Antioch which represent scenes from popular stories of the period or pictures of famous literary or mythical figures. All these mosaic subjects, especially the myths, could be subdivided into a series of pictures each set within a general framework. The Labours of Hercules were often represented, as were the Loves of Zeus, the chief Greek god. Mosaics showing these subjects have also been found in Syria and the Lebanon. One was also found near the Roman theatre at Berytus, modern Beirut.

During the late 3rd and early 4th centuries, the social landscape of the Roman empire was marked by the decline of its cities. The rich and powerful began to retreat to their country estates because Septimus Severus, and the emperors who followed him, exploited the cities financially. The Roman upper class, the so-called *honestiores,* came to reside like feudal lords on their estates, surrounded by their own tenants and servants. There they felt securely removed from the crushing financial demands of the imperial government.

Their villas were decorated with pavements representing their individual and special interests. Since most of their days were spent in farming and hunting, it is these themes that appeared most frequently in their mosaics. One pavement, from the beginning of the 4th century, represents the Four Seasons of the year; between them appears a series of hunting adventures. Another mosaic, known as the Worcester pavement because of its present location in Worcester, Mass., shows eight legendary hunters fighting different beasts.

4.   Piazza Armerina

The most splendid of these villas decorated with mosaics was discovered at Piazza Armerina in Sicily. From a representation of the owner depicted on one of the pavements, it is assumed that this was an imperial villa belonging to Herculius Maximinus, co-emperor of Diocletian (AD 285–305). The villa covers a vast area, most of which was paved with mosaics. The subjects for these can be divided into three categories. The first concerns everything connected with the life and activities of the imperial court. In one of the scenes, we see the arrival of the lord of the estate. He is greeted by servants bearing lighted candles and palm branches. The ecstatic expressions on the faces of the servants show that they considered their master at the very least the equal of a god. The lord's family, his wife and sons, are shown enjoying the pleasure of a bath, surrounded by servants.

The second category is hunting, an important subject in these pavements, which is represented by three different scenes. One, called the "Little Hunt", shows hares sacrificed to Diana, while birds and deer are being caught. The hunt ends in a picnic under a tent, with chicken served on a platter. The dangers of the sport are also shown in the "Little Hunt" pavement — one part of the scene shows a hunt of the wild boars in which one of the hunters is severely wounded.

The second of these three pavements is called the "Big Hunt". It is devoted not to the killing of animals, but rather to catching them and their subsequent transportation for use in the imperial circus. Servants are shown catching wild boars, elephants, rhinoceroses and lions, which are being placed in cages and dragged aboard ships. Other beasts are transported in large wagons. The ship is probably preparing to sail from Africa to Sicily or Rome. On this pavement, the owner of the estate is shown wearing the characteristic round cap of the period. He is surrounded by his friends and servants. In the "Big Hunt" pavement occasional attacks on hunters are also depicted.

The third pavement with a hunting theme shows children (Cupids) imitating the adult activities.

Next to hunting, the circus was this

villa owner's favourite subject. A highly detailed pavement in his villa shows the chariot races at the circus. The charioteers wear the usual four colours representing the four seasons: white, blue, green, and red. The various accidents which were likely to occur during a race are carefully depicted in this mosaic. Finally, the victory of a green chariot is shown — apparently the owner of the villa favoured the green faction.

The same circus scene is represented in another pavement, but in a slightly grotesque fashion. In this second mosaic, children take the place of the charioteers, and deer, geese, flamingoes, doves, and birds replace the horses.

The third of these categories is a group of mosaic pavements representing mythological or symbolical scenes. Among these are very interesting representations of the Labours of Hercules,

A section of the "Big Hunt" pavement, Piazza Armerina

a patron deity of the lord of the villa. Only the great hero's victims are shown: the pavement is strewn with dead and bleeding monsters, animals, and heroes, all defeated by the invincible Hercules.

He himself is shown only outside the pavement, where he is being crowned by the goddess Victory. Other pavements of this type show the punishment of King Lycurgus, who dared to doubt the power of the god Dionysus, and the monster Cyclops who was blinded by Odysseus. These are symbolic representations of the terrible fate which was in store for enemies of the establishment and of the emperor.

5. *Britain*

Roman mosaics in Britain seem to have flourished very late, almost at the very end of the Roman art period. There were three main centres of mosaic art in this province: one at Brough-on-the-Humber in the East Riding of Yorkshire, another at Dorchester in Dorset, and the third at Cirencester in Gloucestershire.

Most of the mosaics belonged to villas in Yorkshire or south-western England and can be dated to about AD 300–70. While the composition of the pavements follows the usual subdivision into panels separated by geometric ornamentation, the fourth-century mosaics of Britain show a fairly individual style, in which strong influences of the art of the northern peoples, the Vikings as they later came to be called, are noticeable. The subjects depicted were taken largely from Greco-Roman mythology, and include representations of Orpheus charming wild animals with his music and of Bellerophon attacking the beast Chimera.

Two such pavements, one at Hinton St Mary and the other at Frampton, are especially interesting. They combine pagan myths with the monogram of Christ; the mosaic at Hinton St Mary contains the portrait of Christ, the earliest known on a floor mosaic.

The pavement at Brading reflects the teachings of one of the many mystic sects which flourished in the Late Roman period, collectively known as "Gnostics" (those who know). It has a parallel in a pavement in Trier, Germany, which also seems to reflect some mystic rites caught up with the story of Jupiter, Leda and the Dioscuri.

Other mosaics found in Britain indicate the literary interests of the villa owners, such as the representations of the loves of Venus and Aeneas, and the story of Dido, all taken from the epic of the Latin poet Virgil, written four centuries earlier. Besides these specific subjects we find themes common to the whole Roman world, such as circus races (at Horkstow) and hunting scenes, examples of which abound in British mosaics. The rows of animals shown in the pavements at Winterton and Cirencester, with their representations of elephants and lions (hardly likely to be seen in Britain in the 4th century), show how dependent the artists in this remote province were on their mother city, Rome.

Right: Leopard on Maon synagogue pavement
Overleaf left: Menorah on Maon synagogue pavement
Overleaf right: Offering of Isaac, detail from Beth Alpha synagogue pavement

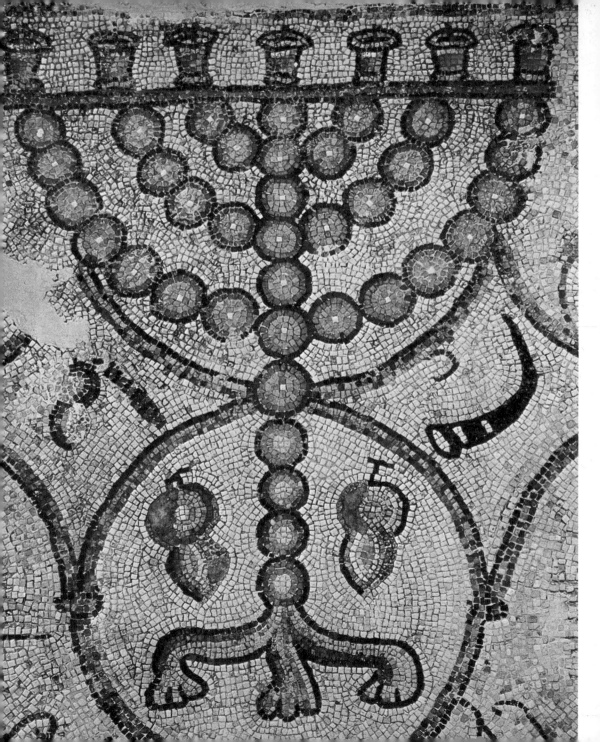

III PAVEMENTS OF THE BYZANTINE WORLD

1. *Antioch*

The later Roman mosaics at Antioch (from the 3rd century onwards), and the mosaics of Roman Germany, Gaul, and Britain, indicate a marked change in style — there is a definite abandonment of the Hellenistic impressionism that Roman artists had adopted in their mosaic pavements.

At a fairly early date, the "conceptual" method of representation made its appearance in the Antioch pavements. This meant that pictures were represented not as they appeared to the eye, but as they were thought of in the mind of the spectator. In one of these mosaics, a lion is shown marching across a field decorated with diagonal lines of flowers. The artist did not hesitate to break up the floral background in order to have his lion walk across it; he paid little attention to the complete integrity of the design. This design, and another showing a row of two-headed ibexes in the margin, are signs of the increasing orientalization of mosaic art. Influences

Left: Pavement from church at Heptapegon

from the Oriental world of the conceptual type of art infiltrated the illusionistic world of Greek art, which was based on perspective and the reproduction of the visual image. Such changes marked the beginning of the evolution of the Byzantine mosaic pavement, which was based on conceptions very different from those of the Greeks and the Romans. The most important change was the abandonment of the traditional plan, in which a group of pictures was represented in perspective depth on the floor, so that the spectator felt as if he were sinking into it. In the Byzantine pavements, the whole floor formed a unity with its subdivisions marked out by medallions or squares. Images were set within these without depth or perspective.

2. *The Great Palace at Constantinople*

This transition is perhaps best observed in the technically excellent mosaics found in the Great Palace. They were dated by archaeological evidence to the middle of the 5th century, but when they were first discovered, there was considerable doubt about their correct date. The workmanship of the mosaics was so good and the subjects so Hellenistic that archaeologists thought they must have belonged to a much earlier period. Archaeological evidence, however, was very clear, and the 5th century date is now generally accepted.

We can assume that the Roman emperors, who had the best technical craftsmanship at their disposal, chose artists who were trained in the old traditions of the Greco-Roman world. This training was applied to the making of the pavements in the corridor which connected the Palace of Constantinople to the Hippodrome. The subjects depicted were purely secular and were not subject to the discipline which governed the decorations in religious buildings. The Constantinople mosaics show a series of idyllic scenes, hunts, and circus representations. These are executed either realistically or by the common Roman practice of showing children imitating their elders. The single pictures are detached from their surroundings and are placed within a uniform white background which serves all of them without distinction.

The ordinary Byzantine pavement, whether secular or religious in theme, was based on an overall scheme of geometric or floral designs. The whole surface of the floor was set within a decorated border, which was either geometrical or formed by garlands of various types of leaves. Different patterns subdivided the floor into areas of equal size, which were circular medallions, squares or other regular shapes. The spaces left within the pavement were very often decorated by a series of designs which together formed a whole. Some pavements showed the Labours of the Months, representing each month in its particular characteristic activity. The Four Seasons were also depicted, as were other subjects which could be divided into a fixed number of units and still form a whole.

In turn, the whole floor formed an integrated surface. There were no perspectival "pits" as there were in Roman pavements. Because the entire floor pattern was basically geometrical, it could be applied to rooms of any size. The pattern could be terminated or extended at will, and it could be continued indefinitely.

3. *The Holy Land*

Byzantine mosaics spread far and wide over the whole Roman empire, but Palestine, the Holy Land of both

Christians and Jews, held a special position in this development. More mosaics have been found proportionally in Byzantine Palestine than in any other province of the Roman empire.

Among the earliest Byzantine mosaics found in this area is a pavement at Beth Govrin, south-west of Jerusalem, which was probably once part of a Constantinian villa. The Four Seasons are represented, and in the centre are square panels in which beasts of prey face their victims — lions, tigers, and bears against sheep, cattle, and deer. In this work the hunters and the hunted dwell together in peace, as they are supposed to have done in Messianic times. Along the edges of the pavement, the owner of the villa is shown starting out on a hunt. On the way, he is greeted by a shepherd tending his flock and then, on horseback or on foot, he attacks various savage animals. Finally, he returns home victorious.

A number of pavements found at sites between Jerusalem and Gaza, including the one at Beth Govrin, may be the work of the Gaza School — a group of artists who worked in the 6th century at Gaza in south-western Palestine. Their work will be further illustrated when church mosaics are discussed later in this chapter. The so-called Armenian Pavement at Jerusalem is the work of this school. It was found near the Damascus Gate and is still at its original site.

In 1900, another interesting mosaic was found near the Armenian pavement outside the Damascus Gate. This pavement is significant because it shows that representations from Greek mythology were used by the later Byzantines — if they could be interpreted symbolically. It shows Orpheus, the mythical Greek singer, surrounded by animals and a satyr, the woodland god of Greek mythology. Below are the images of two women, Theodosia and Georgia, who were most likely the donors of the pavement. It is now at the Archaeological Museum in Istanbul.

At Beth Shean, south of the Sea of Galilee, a monastery was discovered which was founded by a woman named Mary at the end of the 6th century. The whole courtyard of the monastery is paved with mosaics. In the centre is a representation of the Labours of the Months, adjusted to the seasons of the hot Jordan Valley. The grape harvest, for example, is advanced from September to July. In the centre of this mosaic are personifications of the Sun and the Moon.

Another interesting pavement was found in a monastery near Mount Nebo, east of the Jordan. It shows the sanctuary of the Jerusalem Temple, probably the one dating from the time of Solomon.

Sacrificial animals are being led to the altar, and the appropriate Biblical verses are included.

4. *Church Mosaics*

Byzantine mosaics, like most artistic and literary manifestations of this culture, mainly served religious art. A certain period of time had to pass, however, before figurative pavements were admitted to churches at all.

The early Christians considered the various representations of pagan Greek mythology shocking and immoral, and refused to allow these themes to appear in their church mosaics. In private homes, however, Greek mythological themes continued to be used well into the Byzantine period. It is understandable that the Christians refused to use anything which reminded them of paganism and instead preferred simple geometric patterns. Only rarely are church pavements found which are anything but geometrical design. One such case is the fourth-century pavement of the basilica at Aquileia in Italy, on which figurative scenes were found.

In the pavements of early churches, the symbol of the cross was still used, but even this was frowned upon by the religious authorities. In AD 427, the Byzantine Emperor Theodosius II (408–50) issued a decree forbidding its use in the decoration of pavements. We find many cases in which crosses were removed from pavements or covered over by mosaics with other designs. The cross was occasionally used inside churches, but only in rooms to which access was restricted to ordained priests.

The more splendid Byzantine basilicas were not paved with mosaics at all. Instead, they were paved with marble slabs set in various designs. The art of mosaics was left to the humble village churches in the provinces. Most of the mosaics from early churches in Byzantine Palestine are of geometrical design, although there are occasional symbolic representations.

In the middle of the 5th century, however, a change of policy took place. From that time onwards, figurative mosaics were included in the overall scheme of church decoration, which followed a definite programme on ceilings, walls, and floors. Within that scheme, the "earthly paradise" was left for the pavement, which most often showed scenes of village life.

One of the earliest and finest mosaics of this type was found in the church at Heptapegon (the "Seven Sources"). This site, called *et-Tabgha* in Arabic, is situated on the shore of the Sea of Galilee. According to Christian tradition, it is here that the miracle of the

Scene representing a basket of Loaves and two Fishes, Heptapegon

Loaves and Fishes took place. On the pavement below the altar table a basketful of loaves with a fish on either side is depicted. On two sides of the church, the artist added pavements with representations of the animals and flowers found in the vicinity of the Sea of Galilee. A pattern of buildings and trees is shown on the surface of the pavement in the usual Byzantine manner. The whole picture is done without proportion or shading. Within this overall pattern, we find illustrations of a device used for measuring the rise and fall of the water level, usually called a Nilometer. The quality of the pavement is excellent and it must have attracted many visitors, which probably helped to spread the use of mosaic art to other churches in Palestine as well as to other countries.

Within a period of about two centuries (from AD 450 to the time of the Arab conquest in 640), mosaic pavements were made in nearly a thousand churches and other buildings all over Palestine, on both sides of the Jordan. One of the most famous of these is the mosaic map on the pavement of a church at Medeba, east of the Dead Sea, which has provided us with the first known map of the Holy Land. The city of Jerusalem, in the centre of the map, is shown as it appeared in the Byzantine period. Other cities are depicted around it and various Biblical locations are represented with names and identification. There is also a remarkable impressionistic representation of the Jordan River and the Dead Sea. The topography and geography of Biblical Palestine are shown in detail. The map is oriented to the east, as was the practice in antiquity. The eastern

Detail of Heptapegon pavement

desert is on the upper part of the map and the sea in the west is set below. The Medeba map also includes part of the Nile valley — it was probably meant to represent the whole Biblical world of the Old Testament, from Phoenicia to Egypt.

Byzantine artists liked to use a vine trellis pattern as a basic decoration on their pavements. Although this design was inherited from Roman times, it is nevertheless found in many church mosaics. The branches of the vine formed a series of round medallions, each of which was filled in with a representation of village life such as a hunting scene, the vintage and so on. Sometimes a sly, humorous touch was introduced. At Qabr Hiram, south of Tyre, for instance, a mosaic shows an angry housewife pursuing a fox who has stolen one of her hens.

At some later period, perhaps after the start of Arab rule, the Christians were forced to remove all images of living beings — men and animals — from church floors. These had to be replaced with geometric designs or with plain pavements in which the mosaic cubes were reused in no apparent order. This brought about a very curious phenomenon; one that can be observed at Khirbet Asida, one of the many churches between Jerusalem and Hebron.

Apparently, the order to remove all images of animals and birds was duly received at this church. But instead of removing the animals completely, an unknown artist transformed them into pictures of flowers, which were not regarded as living beings and were therefore permitted to appear. On this mosaic, a lion whose tail forms a long and wavy yellow flower is a very curious sight indeed. His mane and head have been shaped into another flower, while his four legs form flower stems. The contour of the lion's body can still be clearly recognized, and this converted beast forms a floral ensemble not to be found in any botanical handbook!

In the churches at Gerasa, east of the Jordan, Nilotic scenes were used as mosaic subjects. These included representations of Alexandria, the city "Egypt" (Memphis), and other towns. A similar representation has been found at Haditha near Lydda.

The school of mosaic artists working in the 6th century at Gaza in southwestern Palestine deserves special mention. These artists apparently were employed by both synagogues and churches. They produced at least three, and perhaps four or five, church pavements. One of these was found accidentally in 1917 by Australian soldiers who had come to Palestine to serve in the British army under General Allenby,

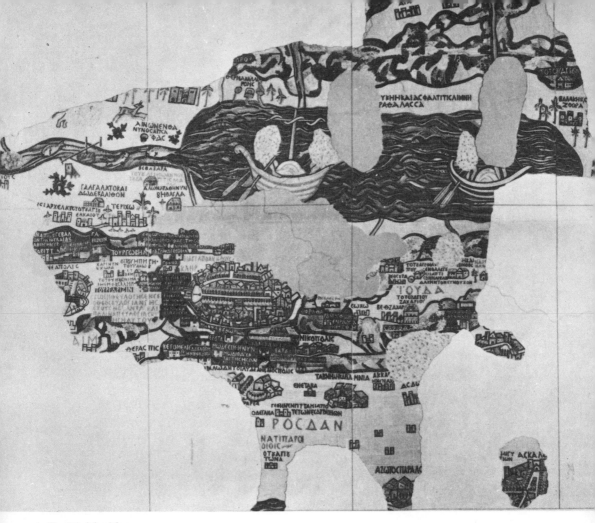

The Medeba Map

then engaged in chasing the Ottoman Turks out of the Holy Land. The pavement, dated to AD 561, was found at Shellal. It was later transferred to Canberra in Australia and was reset in the War Memorial there — it is the only Byzantine pavement ever to be moved so far from its place of origin. The Shellal pavement is based on the vine trellis pattern — there are five medallions in a row. The central apse in the picture is filled with various offerings for the altar, such as baskets and vases filled with fruit. Animals are arranged symmetrically in pairs on both sides of the central row of medallions.

5. *Synagogue Mosaics*

The Gaza School artists also worked on a special kind of mosaic found mainly, although not exclusively, in ancient Palestine; the mosaic pavements for synagogues. Jews had used mosaics since the first century of the Christian era, and possibly even before that time.

The earliest dated Jewish mosaics are those found in the Herodian palace at Masada on the shore of the Dead Sea

Scene of village life, Beth Shean monastery pavement

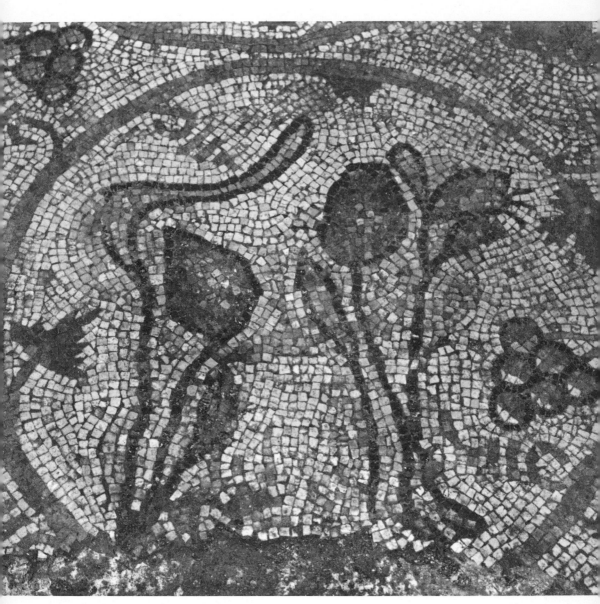

Lion transformed into flowers, Khirbet Asida

and in Herodian houses in Jerusalem. Since the pavements of the Masada palace must date to the time that it was built, we can assume that they were made before 30 BC. They are Hellenistic in conception, but have two particular distinctions: first, all images of living beings are avoided, because the Jewish rabbis in the time of the Second Temple did not allow such representations; and second, the commonly used Hellenistic patterns were adapted into Jewish designs. This is particularly true in the mosaic which shows a representation of the Seven Kinds of Fruit with which the Holy Land was blessed. Thus we find the vine scroll or traditional palm pattern together with figs, pomegranates, and the like.

When the use of mosaic art was resumed by the Jews in the 4th century for the ornamentation of their synagogues, the medium underwent a complete transformation. Apparently, the prohibition against the use of images of living beings had been modified by then. The rabbis of that period adopted a different interpretation of the Second Commandment, prohibiting idolatrous images. At Beth Shearim, a large cemetery was built around the tomb of the venerated patriarch Judah I. Jews from all over the East were buried there in order to be near this holy tomb. In the courts of one tomb, four dolphins were represented in a mosaic. There also seems to have been a figurative image in the centre, but it has since disappeared.

In the Byzantine period, Jews were forbidden to decorate the exteriors of their synagogues. This prohibition led them to decorate the interiors of the buildings as richly as they could and this included the use of mosaic pavements. As a result, there now exists a series of synagogue pavements from this period, ranging from the early 4th to the 8th centuries. One of the earliest of these pavements was found at Hammath, the site of the natural hot springs just south of the city of Tiberias on the Sea of Galilee. From the 3rd century onwards, Tiberias was the seat of the Jewish patriarchate, as well as a centre of Jewish learning. In the synagogue at Hammath, we find the typical representation of the Zodiac, with the Twelve Signs surrounding an image of the sun. The latter is represented in its pagan shape as Phoebus Apollo, a charioteer driving a four-horsed chariot. In this particular case, the images of the various signs of the Zodiac are strongly influenced by pagan art; they seem to have been derived entirely from the world of Greek and Roman mythology. The symbol of the Virgin, for instance (*Koré* in Greek), is represented as Persephone — the daughter of Demeter, the Greek corn goddess. Persephone is

shown as a veiled woman holding a torch in her hand. The symbol of the Scales is depicted as a king holding a sceptre in one hand and a set of balances in the other. The king is probably Minos or Rhadamantes, one of the dreaded judges of the underworld.

The Hammath-Tiberias synagogue represents an exceptional case of the early figurative synagogue pavement. Jewish mosaic art, however, did not reach its peak until the middle of the 5th century AD. The early fifth-century pavements, such as the one at Caesarea, usually show only geometric designs since Jews, like the early Christians, shunned the pagan type of figurative design. In the synagogue pavements various areas were marked with the names of donors. Beside each name, the size of the area presented to the holy place was noted.

The first synagogue in which figurative representations were used was found at Gerasa, east of the Jordan. Biblical scenes and characters, which as we have seen were forbidden in Christian churches, were generally favoured in synagogues. The synagogue at Gerasa can be dated more or less exactly because it was destroyed before AD 530, when a church was built on its ruins. We can be certain, therefore, that the pavement must have been made before the middle of the 6th century AD. The

most interesting part of this pavement is a panel depicting the animals entering Noah's Ark. We can assume that the images of Noah's sons were also represented on the pavement, because the names "Shem" and "Japhet" are written beside the panel itself. This panel is only the first in a series of biblical scenes which have been found in synagogue pavements, the first of which was made early in the 6th century. They represent a selection of biblical stories from a particular point of view; that is, they illustrate the ways of Providence — the divine salvation offered to humanity, to the Jewish people, or to chosen individuals. The selection of the subjects was based on the texts of certain prayers, especially those offered in times of drought. It included the stories of Noah's Ark, the Offering of Isaac by Abraham, Daniel in the Lion's Den, and similar events.

One of the earliest synagogues of the type described above is, however, slightly different from the others. It was discovered on the seashore near Gaza, and belonged to this harbour city, then called Constantia Maiumas. An inscription dates the pavement to AD 508–9; it was a product of the Gaza school of mosaic artists. The mosaic shows King David dressed in the costume of a Byzantine emperor. He sits, playing his lyre, and is surrounded by various

Left: The Autumn Season, from Zodiac pavement, Hammath-Tiberias

animals, mainly wild beasts. The scene represents David as Orpheus, the mythical Greek singer who charmed wild beasts with his sweet song. In Christian symbolism, Orpheus represented Jesus, who tamed the wild passions of men just as Orpheus tamed the wild beasts. In the same symbolic sense, this pavement in a Jewish synagogue parallels Orpheus and David, the poet and psalmist respectively. The Gaza pavement was discovered in 1965, at which time the Egyptians still occupied Gaza.

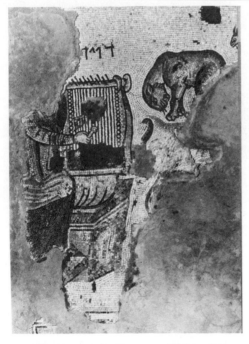

The "David" mosaic, Gaza, note Hebrew letters spelling David

Although the letters of the Hebrew name David (דויד) appear beside the image, Egyptian archaeologists reported that the pavement showed "a female saint playing the lyre".

Another example of a Jewish pavement strongly influenced by Greek mythology was found at Beth Shean in a house owned by a man called Leontis, which adjoined the synagogue. The mosaic shows a Nilotic landscape, a representation of the city of Alexandria, the god of the Nile, a crocodile attacking a cow, and scenes from Homer's Odyssey, such as the encounter between Odysseus and the Sirens. The former is also shown fighting the monster Scylla. This pavement, which dates to the 6th century, indicates that Greek mythology, and the Homeric poems in particular, were still known and appreciated by the Jews of Byzantine Palestine.

The artists of the Gaza School probably worked at Maon, south of Gaza, as well. There a pavement was found in the grounds of Kibbutz Nirim while a road was being built. We are very lucky, in fact, that this mosaic was preserved at all. The labourers who found it at first intended to destroy it, because they did not want to interrupt their work. But, as good democrats, they voted on the decision, and the pavement was saved by a vote of three to two. The Maon synagogue pavement

Part of Maon synagogue pavement (for detail see p. 38)

is particularly interesting because it represents a type of decoration normally found in churches. At the lower end of the pavement stands an amphora, the Greek or Roman two-handled vessel.

From the amphora, a vine trellis develops into circular medallions which contain pairs of animals arranged symmetrically. These face each other across the axial stem. On the stem itself, various offerings are represented: silver vases filled with fruit, a hen laying an egg, a bird in a cage, and so on. This whole scheme of decoration has been interpreted as symbolic; the amphora and the vine trellis represent Paradise and the peacocks flanking it are symbols of immortality. But it is obvious that in this synagogue mosaic, which can be dated to about AD 530, the symbols were not sufficiently religious for the artists or their patrons. Therefore, they added a section of specifically Jewish symbols at the northern part of the pavement — the part which faced Jerusalem. Among these are the seven-branched candlestick, or *menorah;* two lions — one on either side of the *menorah;* two palm trees, and various Jewish ritual objects. These include the *shofar,* a ram's horn used in the synagogue on certain occasions; and the *lulav* and *ethrog* — a palm branch and citrus fruit which are used as part of the ritual at the Feast of Tabernacles. The Maon pavement is astoundingly similar to the one found in the church at Shellal, which is of a slightly later date.

Synagogue pavements, however, tended to be generally geometrical and floral rather than figurative. This was partly because the Jews suffered severe persecutions under the Byzantine government. Since they regarded their suffering as a punishment for laxity, they tended to interpret their laws more rigorously. This included the Second Commandment, which forbade the making of graven images. As a result, we see that in synagogue pavements there was a general and slow retreat from figurative art to floral or geometrical art. At Husifa on Mount Carmel (today the Druse village of Isfiya), a pavement was discovered which depicts a vine trellis and peacocks combined with the Zodiac. In this case, however, the signs of the Zodiac are not always represented by human figures, but sometimes by symbols. In the Husifa mosaic, however, the seasons in each corner are represented by busts of young women surrounded by the appropriate floral symbols.

The pavement of Beth Alpha is probably the most famous of synagogue pavements from Byzantine Palestine. It dates to the years AD 518–27, the reign of the emperor Justin I. The synagogue was a typical village house of prayer — in this remote place the anti-figurative tendency is not yet noticeable. Since Beth Alpha was a small and out-of-the-way village, it was probably not affected by the main trend of development in Jewish mosaics.

The artists who produced this pavement were a man called Marinos and his son Hananiah. Their work followed the classical pattern of a synagogue pavement in the nave of a basilical

Offering of Isaac, Beth Alpha (for detail see p. 39)

building, which is divided into three panels. The Ark of the Law is nearest to the podium, which served as the focus of prayer. The Zodiac is represented in the middle of the pavement, and the biblical scene of the Offering of Isaac is shown at the end nearest the entrance. In the centre of this section, Abraham, dressed in a long robe, is holding the sacrificial knife. Above him, a hand appears from a cloud with the rays of the sun shining behind it. This hand is the symbol of divine power in Jewish and early Christian art. Beside it is the word "Abraham". He holds Isaac with his left hand; Isaac's hands are bound behind his back and the altar with a high flame is behind him. The sacrificial ram which was substituted for Isaac appears tied to a tree in the centre of the picture. To its left are two of Abraham's servants with a donkey. A row of palm trees above the picture indicates the surroundings.

Zodiac in centre of the Beth Alpha synagogue pavement

This panel, as well as the Zodiac panels with images of human beings, is executed in a vigorous and popular style — conceptual art of a very characteristic type. Every detail of the story is explained as clearly as possible while little attention is paid to the visual aspect of the figures. The Virgin, who appeared as the *Koré* of Greek mythology at Hammath-Tiberias, is shown here as the Byzantine empress or a Jewish bride seated on a throne. In the corners of the pavement at Beth Alpha, there are images of the Four Seasons, represented as beautiful maidens holding floral symbols.

The same artists who executed this pavement worked in a very different style at the near by city of Scythopolis. This may be due to the fact that the synagogue there was a Samaritan one. The Samaritans observed the rulings of the Torah and the written law much more strictly than the Jews; they did not interpret it by way of the Oral Law as did the main body of Jews.

The synagogue next in the line of development was found at Hammath Gader, the site of hot springs and a bathing place below the city of Gadara, which was for some time a fashionable resort. At this site, as at Maon, no images of human beings were used, and the beasts depicted are limited to two symbolic lions flanking an inscription.

All the other ornamentation is floral or geometrical.

At Susiya near Hebron, another pavement was recently uncovered. Originally, it contained the images of Daniel in the Lions' Den and a Zodiac. These had been removed, however, and only two deer flanking the Ark of the Law remain. Similarly, the scene of Daniel in the Lions' Den on the mosaic in the synagogue of Na'aran near Jericho ('Ain Duk in Arabic) was not allowed a panel of its own. Instead, it was moved over nearer the Ark. Characteristically, the Jews themselves seem to have removed the images of men and beasts from this pavement. Only the written inscriptions explaining the signs of the Zodiac were left intact. To the Jews of that time, the writing was sacred because it was the vehicle of the Scripture. The images themselves, however, were offensive and had to be removed. The same tendency is noticeable in a synagogue at Jericho, where the pavement bears only the representation of the Ark of the Law, the seven-branched candlestick, and a floral carpet.

The end of this development can be observed in a synagogue of the 6th century at Engedi. Although one part of the pavement shows birds arranged symmetrically around a geometrical motif, in another section the names of the Zodiac signs have been substituted

A mosaic in green, gold and brown from Khirbet Mefjer

for their images. It was left to the writing, therefore, to carry off the whole effect. The Engedi synagogue was probably the last to be paved in Jewish Palestine during the Byzantine period.

6. *Mosaics in the Arab Period*

Geometrical pavements continued to be produced during the Arab period (AD 633–1099), under the rule of Islam. In the eighth-century palace of an Umayyad Caliph (perhaps Hisham) at Khirbet Mefjer, north of Jericho, the geometrical motif was used in a very complicated manner which recalls the later arabesque decorations. At Mefjer, there is one exception to this rule. In a bath near the throne room is a very fine pavement with the Tree of Life in the centre and a lion attacking a group of gazelles beneath it. All this work is done in a highly naturalistic manner. This is the last of the Umayyad pavements known to us. From the remains at Khirbet Mefjer, especially the stucco sculptures, we know that the Umayyads were generally lax about observing the Islamic prohibition against using images of man or beast, while the dynasty which followed, that of the Abbasids, was much stricter. As far as we know, there are no later pavements of this kind in existence.

At this point we leave mosaic pavements and proceed to a very different kind of mosaic art — wall mosaics. This medium was used to decorate the inside walls, the domes, and sometimes even the outer walls of churches and occasionally mosques as well. In general, the use of wall mosaics in antiquity must have been much more common than we can judge at present. A wall mosaic could be preserved only if the wall to which it was applied remained standing. In order to find wall mosaics we must — ideally — locate buildings still in their original state of use, or buildings which were reused for another purpose, escaped destruction, and still remain intact. Mosaic pavements had a much better chance of escaping the ravages of time and were preserved even though the buildings in which they were contained were destroyed. Indeed, the rubble formed a protective covering.

As we have seen earlier, the earliest known example of the application of mosaics to walls was found at Erech (Warka) in Mesopotamia and dates to about 2600 BC. Much later, at Pompeii, wall mosaics were used mainly in buildings connected with the use of water, such as fountains or *nymphea*. It is easy to understand why mosaics were used in this context — water could not damage, or seep through, mosaic walls.

1. *Early Church Mosaics*

The earliest wall mosaic, after those found at Pompeii, depicts Sylvanus, the Italian god of the woods. This work, found at Ostia, dates to the 3rd century AD. An image of Christ from about the same period was also discovered in a crypt below St Peter's in Rome. This third-century work shows Jesus represented as a sun god in a chariot, with rays shining about his head. It is interesting to note that the earliest surviving Christian wall mosaics imitate to a large extent the pavement decorations of the same buildings.

The earliest Christian mosaics have been preserved in the underground

Birds, trees and decorative objects, Church of St Constanza, Rome

crypts of churches. In Italy a splendid series of church wall mosaics still survives, mainly because Islam never became the religion of that country. The churches, therefore, were left standing and escaped the destruction which befell them in Greece and Turkey.

One example of pagan influence is the mosaics in the church at Santa Constanza, Rome, built in AD 320–40, which served as a mausoleum for the imperial family of Constantine. On the domes and ceilings appear mosaic renderings of vine trellises or of the floor of the "unswept house" *(asoratos oikos)*, discussed under "Hellenistic Mosaics". Various objects such as branches, jugs, birds and so on are shown in wild disorder on one of these mosaics. In another, on the ceiling, there is a vine trellis curling around the bust of a woman. Scenes of a distinct pagan character, including Cupids and dancers, some of them half-naked, appear along the edges.

The true Christian style of wall mosaic may be said to begin with those found in two basilicas in Rome — Santa Pudenziana from the late 4th century, and Santa Maria Maggiore from the 5th century. In both cases, the arch over the altar and the eastern basilica wall were used to portray Christ in his glory, surrounded by his apostles. (An alternative subject of these early wall mosaics was the depiction of scenes from the life of Christ, arranged to resemble a triumphal arch.)

In the Santa Pudenziana basilica, the holy cities of Bethlehem and Jerusalem are shown; the birthplace of Jesus and the site of the Crucifixion respectively. The work is realistic in style — the buildings shown within the walls of the two cities include the Church of the Holy Sepulchre and the Church of the Nativity. These are depicted more or less as they really looked at the time. In the Santa Maria Maggiore basilica, however, and in later churches as well, the Holy Cities were represented by schematic images. Heavenly Jerusalem and heavenly Bethlehem are shown with golden walls, richly encrusted with jewels.

At Santa Maria Maggiore, scenes from the Old Testament decorate the walls of the nave of the basilica. These appear over the columns separating the nave from the side aisles and below the clerestory windows. In the later Middle Ages, these images formed part of the *Biblica Pauperum,* the "Bible of the Poor". The scenes were given this name because they illustrated the stories of the Bible to the illiterate poor.

On the long walls of Santa Maria Maggiore, we find the story of the Old Testament. The section that has been preserved begins with the scene from

Genesis XIV, when Abraham meets with Melchizedek, King of Salem, and ends with Joshua. The scenes are executed in an impressionistic manner resembling Hellenistic paintings, with shadows and highlights emphasizing the sculptural qualities of the bodies. The very rich use of colour recalls the tachist school of impressionistic painting which flourished in the 19th century. Since mosaics are composed of small units of uniform colour throughout, they closely resemble the tachist or pointillist style, which is also based on dots of uniform colour.

The Old Testament scenes in the basilica at Santa Maria Maggiore and other churches must have originated in illuminated manuscripts of Bible stories, which included elaborate illustrations. They were probably first created by the Jews who lived in Alexandria. Later they were copied by Jews and Christians alike, as we can see from the frescoes of the synagogue at Dura-Europos, an ancient city on the Euphrates, and in the early catacombs.

2. *The Mosaics of Ravenna*

The lively style of illustration found at Santa Maria Maggiore was still used in the 5th and 6th centuries at Ravenna in Italy, although it was gradually supplanted by the much more solemn Byzantine style. In the 5th century, Ravenna was selected as the capital of the western empire, since Rome was no longer safe. The city was originally a harbour on the Adriatic Sea and during the early Roman Empire, a Roman fleet was stationed there. But the River Po gradually filled the harbour with silt and, during the Byzantine period, a new port was built at some distance from the city. Today Ravenna is several miles from the sea.

In the 5th century, however, the harbour was still within walking distance of the town. On the land side, Ravenna was surrounded by swamps, which made it safe from attack in that direction. For this reason, the emperors of the declining Western Empires selected this city as their place of residence. Later on, in the 6th century, the Gothic kings of Italy lived there. After Justinian reconquered Italy, the Byzantine governors of Italy came to live in Ravenna. Luckily for the history of wall mosaics, Ravenna was a very poor city and did not develop much during the Renaissance or later periods. Since the inhabitants could not afford to build new churches, they kept the old ones intact and thus the wall mosaics were preserved. The value of these works was recognized in the 19th century and the mosaics were repaired and recorded at that time.

In the Ravenna mosaics, we notice a

Vault decoration, star studded sky, Mausoleum of Galla Placida

transition from the original blue background of earlier wall mosaics — first to a green background and then to the gold which is so characteristic of Byzantine wall mosaics. The earliest mosaics found at Ravenna are in the mausoleum of the Empress Galla Placida, which was built about the

The Emperor Justinian, San Vitale, Ravenna

middle of the 5th century. Against the blue background are realistic images of the Saints — Peter, Paul, and Lawrence — to whom the church was dedicated, as well as a representation of Christ as the good shepherd. The vault of the mausoleum imitates the sky; it is covered with stars against a blue background.

Another wall mosaic at Ravenna is found in a church called St Apollinare Nuovo, which was a new church built for the patron saint of the city. It was actually the palace church of the Gothic kings, which was later rebuilt when the Byzantines occupied the town. The mosaics, therefore, date to after AD 526.

The clerestory wall of St Apollinare Nuovo is covered with figures of saints. The male saints are on one side, the

Overleaf: The Empress Theodora and her retinue, San Vitale, Ravenna

female saints on the other. All are holding symbols of their holiness. The procession of male saints is advancing towards Christ on a throne, while the females move towards the Virgin Mary. She is also seated on a throne and is holding the Christ child in her arms. Both processions are walking through fields of lilies, and palm trees appear in between the figures. These flowers and trees are symbols of Paradise which also recall the Holy Land.

On one side of the church is a series of mosaic panels, each one metre square, which depict the miracles performed by Christ. On the other side, the Passion and the Crucifixion in Jerusalem are represented. These mosaics are set very high on the walls above the scenes of the processions of the saints, but they must once have been placed much lower down, as they can barely be seen in their present position.

The most beautiful mosaics at Ravenna are found in the Church of San Vitale, which was built and completed before AD 547. Biblical scenes were still used, though not prominently; among those depicted are Abel and Melchizedek, the Offering of Isaac, the three angels with Abraham, Moses receiving the Law, and the Prophets Isaiah and Jeremiah.

Against a green background, there is a symbolic vault decorated with acanthus scrolls and garlands, with the symbol of the lamb in the centre. Four angels hold it up in the manner of the Four Seasons pavement found at Antioch. Above the altar is a representation of Christ, on the semi-dome of the apse. He is no longer shown as the Good Shepherd, as in the mausoleum of Empress Galla Placida, but as Christ *"Pantocrator"*. He is seated on a blue globe which is flanked by two angels. St Vitalis, to whom the church was dedicated, is shown on one side of Christ and on the other side the archbishop is offering the church itself to Christ (see p. 77).

On each side of the apse of the church is a famous mosaic scene. On one side is depicted the Emperor Justinian and his court, and on the other is the Empress Theodora with her ladies. The figures are shown against a gold background, which is a characteristic feature of Byzantine mosaics. The figures face the spectator; their elongated bodies and large wide-eyed faces already convey the "spiritual look" of Oriental art. This look is of special interest in the case of Theodora, who is shown with a halo as are her companions and the saints. We notice that, although many of the figures have one foot placed upon the foot of the person beside them, the effect is one of weightlessness — they do not seem to feel any pressure. The Empress is shown on her way to church accom-

Right: The Emperor Leo IV worshiping Christ, Aya Sofia

panied by the ladies of her court while an official obligingly holds aside a curtain for her. Apart from being splendid works of art, the portraits are of great historical interest.

3. *The Mosaics of Greece, Venetia and Constantinople*

In Constantinople, the capital of the Byzantine empire, no wall mosaics have been preserved from earlier than the 9th century because of the iconoclasts. The iconoclastic movement, which prevailed in eighth- to ninth-century Byzantium, was directed against the adoration of images. Although many of the churches later fell into Moslem hands, not all of them were destroyed. In several of them, such as the great church at Constantinople — the Aya Sofia — the mosaics were covered over with plaster or stucco. Fortunately, this can be peeled off and thus the mosaics can sometimes be recovered.

When the iconoclastic movement abated, wall mosaics were again applied in some of the churches at Constantinople, first of all in the Church of the Holy Wisdom (Aya Sofia), the principal church in the capital of the Byzantine empire.

Above the entrance of the church proper, the Emperor Leo is shown bowing down before Christ on His throne. Over a side gate is a picture of the Virgin Mary. To one side of her, the Emperor Constantine is shown offering the city of Constantinople. On the other side, the church itself is offered by the Emperor Justinian. Various imperial donors appear with Christ, Mary, and the saints in the gallery. The interior mosaics of the building are gradually being uncovered; they seem to follow the general style of the other scenes.

Because of the troubles brought by the iconoclasts and the transformation of churches into mosques after the Ottoman conquest of Constantinople in 1453 — and the consequent obliteration of the Christian mosaics — we are obliged to look for examples of Byzantine church mosaics in the provinces (especially in Greece) where the village churches remained largely undisturbed.

Here, a definite scheme of decoration developed which was based on theological as well as artistic considerations.

Right: Duck, 6th century pavement, Hammath-Tiberias
Overleaf left and right: Secular art, 5th century(?) mosaic pavements. Great palace of the Emperors, Constantinople

Above: Christ Pantocrator with St Vitalis and the Archbishop Eclesius. Church of San Vitale, Ravenna

Left: Man playing the flute to his dog on Beth Shean monastery pavement

The dome over the transept of the church was devoted to an impressive picture of Christ Pantocrator, the Ruler of the World. The portrait of Christ, as a judge of the living and the dead, looked down sternly on the sinners as they assembled below in the church. The half-dome behind the apse and the altar was filled in with the figure of the Virgin Mary as the Mother of God, holding the Christ child in her arms. She represents the hope of salvation. In the pendentives — the four triangles descending from the dome — four scenes from the life of Christ are represented: the Nativity at Bethlehem, the Baptism in the Water of the Jordan, the Crucifixion, and the Visit to Limbo — the forecourt of Hell. Christian tradition places the visit to Limbo between the Crucifixion and the Resurrection.

Some of the finest mosaics of this type (from the second part of the 11th century) are to be found in the Monastery Church of Daphni, not far from Athens. They are elegantly designed, richly coloured, and skilfully composed. In the interior of the church, the isolated figures and biblical scenes are arranged according to the fixed Byzantine scheme. In the dome, there is a colossal bust of Christ Pantocrator, surrounded by prophets. In the vault are the archangels Michael and Gabriel. The Virgin Mary is shown enthroned in

the apse, and to the north and south, in the transepts, are various groups of martyrs. There are also gospel scenes in the transepts, as well as in the corners of the dome, and in the vestibule. These include the regular series of New Testament scenes: the Birth of the Virgin, the Salutation, the Nativity of Christ at Bethlehem, the Adoration of the Magi, the Presentation of Christ in the Temple, the Transfiguration, the Entry into Jerusalem, the Crucifixion, the Descent into Hell, the Incredulity of St Thomas, and the Death of the Virgin. The mosaics thus depict the entire story of the Gospel and the Acts of the Apostles.

The next mosaics, in chronological order, are the famous works of the Basilica of San Marco in Venice, which also date from the 11th century. Here, the interest is concentrated on the mosaics of the narthex, or vestibule of the church. The Finnish scholar Tikkonen was the first to notice that these derived from an early illuminated manuscript related to the Cotton Bible. This Bible, an old Byzantine manuscript, belonged to the Cotton family of England and was partially destroyed by fire in the 18th century. Fortunately, copies had been made of some of its drawings before the work was lost. The mosaics of San Marco are derived from the first books of the Old Testament,

The Empress Irene, Aya Sofia

Christ Pantocrator, the Church of Daphni

The Nativity, the Church of Daphni

Genesis and Exodus. They reproduce the pictures and stories depicted and told by Byzantine masters who followed the style of earlier manuscripts.

However, there is one detail in which the San Marco mosaics differ from the earlier Christian manuscripts and their Jewish prototypes. Following the Jewish custom in the ancient manuscripts, the power of God was represented simply by a hand outstretched from heaven. In this church, however, God is represented by the figure of a youthful Christ. This stems from the concept that since Jesus was the son of God, he must have resembled God the Father.

The San Marco mosaics, as mentioned above, depict the complete stories of Genesis and Exodus. The scenes include several panels showing the Creation of the World; the stories of Adam and Eve, Cain and Abel, Noah's Ark, Abraham, Joseph, and Moses; and the events in the wilderness. Among these, we also find Joseph storing wheat in the pyramids, which were thought, at that time, to be storehouses built for the collection of the produce from the Seven Fat Years in Pharaoh's dream. Although the Venetians had access to Egypt and knew what the pyramids looked like, the pyramids in the mosaics at San Marco are somewhat different from reality.

On the island of Torcello, near Venice, is an interesting basilica with wall mosaics which are more or less contemporary to those at San Marco. The Virgin Mary stands alone in the apse against a gold background; she is holding the Christ child in one arm. Below her, the twelve apostles are arranged in hierarchical order. St Peter is at the far right, while St Paul is recognizable by his beard and bald head. On the opposite side is a very interesting representation of Hell — Satan and his minions are shown all in blue. We are reminded that, as in the earlier mosaics at Ravenna, blue is the colour symbolizing sin and evil. Red, the colour of blood, is the symbol of redemption and salvation. Thus, in the mosaics in the Church of St Apollinare Nuovo at Ravenna, where Christ stands between the sheep and the goats, the bad element — the goats — are depicted in blue, as is the Angel of Death who accompanies them. The Angel of Life is shown in red. The reason for these colour symbols is very straightforward. The people of the Middle Ages suffered much more from cold than from heat. Their houses were not properly heated, and therefore they imagined Hell to be a frozen place, not the flaming inferno imagined in later ages. Dante also represents Hell as frozen, with Satan sitting at the very bottom among blocks of ice.

Virgin and Child, Basilica of Torcello

Theodoros Metechites the donor, with model of the Church of Kahrie Jami

In the basilica at Torcello, it is interesting to note that bishops, kings, and unbelievers like Mohammed are pictured among the wicked sinners who are writhing among the fires of hell in the clutches of various devils.

The southern Italian island of Sicily always had close relations with Byzantium, and these continued even under the rule of the Norman kings, from Roger I onwards. The chapels of the Norman rulers at Monreale and at Palermo (the Capella Palatina) were,

therefore, richly decorated by Byzantine artists. At Monreale, a series of Old Testament events are taken as parallels to the New Testament. The various figures are shown in medieval dress; thus the carpenters working on Noah's Ark are shown as if they actually lived in the time when the mosaic was made.

Let us now return to Constantinople. The mosaics in the early thirteenth-century church of the Pammakaristos (now the Mosque of Fetiye Jami) in Constantinople also show Christ and the Apostles. The expression of Christ is now mild and gentle and the positions of the Apostles are skilfully varied. The quality of this work is further proof of the originality and artistic feeling which was revived in Byzantium during the last stages of its existence.

One of the finest examples of the Byzantine mosaic art is found at the Church of Kahrie Jami at Constantinople. These mosaics appear in the monastery of Chora ("in the country"), that is, outside the walls. The monastery itself must have been built before the construction of the wall of Constantinople. These walls, which now encircle the city, were built by Theodosius II, in the first half of the 5th century. The monastery was redecorated with mosaics by order of Theodoros Metechites, the Treasurer of the Byzantine empire between the years 1310 and 1320. In the wall over the gate, between the inner narthex and the church, the donor is shown in a high, turban-like headdress of white striped with red; a gold tunic, and a green flowered mantle. He is kneeling before Christ on his throne and is holding a model of the church. Otherwise, the mosaics depict two cycles representing the Life of Christ and the Life of the Virgin. There are episodes from the Life of Mary, such as the prayer of Joachim and Anna, the Nativity, and the presentation at the Temple. The Annunciation is shown, as well as many portrayals of the saints. These mosaics show an extraordinary feeling for colour and a naturalistic rendering of familiar scenes. These stylistic details gave way to the idea that the mosaics were dependent on the Italian artists of the early Renaissance, although there is no outright proof for this assumption. In the inner narthex, there is a cycle of the history of the Virgin inspired by an apocryphal *Protoevangelium* of James which the mosaic follows scene by scene. In the outer narthex are scenes from the Life of Christ.

In the church itself, only one mosaic has been preserved — the scene depicting the death of the Virgin — but there must have been mosaic scenes of the Passion and the Crucifixion as well. Other discoveries in this church have been made by carefully peeling off the covering affixed by the Turks from the mosaics and the stones. The other artistic features of the church are the frescoes, likewise uncovered, which are also very interesting. They portray, among other scenes, the Last Judgement and Christ's Descent into Hell.

The mosaics of Kahrie Jami show evidence of true originality. The architecture, as well as the ornamental borders which frame the mosaics, is still entirely Byzantine in style, as are the conventional landscapes shown. But in all other aspects this church typifies the renaissance of Byzantine art. Although the general rules of Byzantine paintings are still observed, the figures no longer seem as rigid as they did in the earlier wall mosaics. A sense of movement begins to make itself felt. These mosaics lead us to expect a breakthrough towards livelier representative art, similar to the Italian Renaissance style. (The earliest Italian Renaissance artists, starting with Giotto, all began with the same Byzantine prototype.) But in 1453, the Turks conquered Constantinople and put an end to these expectations. Byzantine mosaic art ends more or less with the works at the Church of Kahrie Jami.

If we consider Byzantine mosaics as a whole, we should first of all note that they were planned so as to make full use of the artistic opportunities presented by the shape of the Byzantine basilica. In most cases, the mosaics were applied to curved surfaces and, as a result, there are some very unexpected lighting effects. In one area, the gold background glitters, while in another it is thrown into shadow. The colours are extraordinarily vivid because of the unchanging nature of the material used. Also, the artists used occasional technical tricks, such as reversing the gold cubes to show the muted reverse side instead of their shiny front surfaces. In this way, a uniform effect was avoided and the whole background became more vivid.

Aesthetically, Byzantine wall mosaics represent a reversal of the Greek standards of illusionistic classical art. They follow the principles which were first elaborated upon in the Orient, such as the theory of hierarchical proportion. According to this theory, the more important figures were depicted as larger in size than the others. Emphasis was also placed on the human figure, which meant that natural features or buildings in the background bore no relation to their actual size. The figures are elongated and there was a definite accent on the more prominent parts of the body such as the head and eyes, which were often enlarged to give a "spiritual" message. Care was taken never to obscure the main figures, such as Christ, the Virgin, the saints, or an emperor. All images were arranged according to their importance, with the principal character in full view, while all the figures faced the spectator. The heads of the figures in the background all appeared at the same height. Because of their frontal position, the figures seemed to be following the spectator with their eyes. In this way, they established spiritual contact with the believers who observed them.

Byzantine wall mosaics, in general, are excellent examples of the metaphysical, unearthly essence of Byzantine art. The images are not realistic portrayals of human beings, but rather representations of certain conceptions and ideas. On the mosaic in the church at Daphni, for instance, Christ is shown as a thin, emaciated figure with very deep-set eyes and lined cheeks. Both Christ and the Virgin Mary are shown as rulers seated on thrones, and are dressed in imperial robes. The only reminders of the older, more realistic style are the sandals worn by Christ. Mary, on the other hand, is shown wearing the red shoes and jewelled headdress of an empress. Of course, the wall mosaics of the Byzantine period followed the rules laid down by the Church for the painting of sacred images. All figures were shown fully clad, and not a hint of their body contours was apparent beneath the rich folds of their clothing. Nevertheless, the Byzantine artists succeeded in creating magnificent works of art. Because they were bound by certain rules, they had to exercise their artistic ingenuity to create a compromise between their artistic feelings and the rules imposed by their Church.

Nevertheless, Byzantine mosaics appear to us as the precursors of certain trends of modern art. Since the principles of perspective and illusion which dominated European art from the Renaissance to the 20th century have been abandoned, Byzantine mosaics have come to be recognized and appreciated.

V THE TECHNIQUE AND PRESERVATION OF MOSAICS

1. Technique

There are definite differences between the technique of mosaic pavements and that of wall mosaics. Both, however, demand the preparation of a solid foundation. A detailed description of the proper way to lay the foundation of a mosaic pavement has been left to us by the Roman architect Vitruvius, who lived in the time of the emperor Augustus (27 BC-AD 14). Three foundation layers were involved, the first being a deep layer of rough pebbles. This was covered with a second layer of cement mixed with brick fragments. The third level was a fine layer of ground bricks and cement into which the mosaic cubes (tesserae) were inserted. The same rule applies, in principle, to wall mosaics. Here too a layer of thick cement was applied to the wall with nails to hold it in place. This was followed by a thin layer of cement over which yet another thin layer served as the foundation for the stones themselves.

The material used for early mosaic pavements was most often natural stones. In most Mediterranean countries, stones could supply all the required variants of red, orange, yellow, black, some blues and greens — such as grey-blue or olive-green — and white or off-white. For example, the mosaic of Hammeh, found near Beth Shean, contains two shades of yellow; two of orange; two of pink; four of red, from brick-red to purple; three shades of grey; three shades of blue; and four shades of green. In this mosaic eleven colours were used — in twenty-four shades.

The only colours not supplied by nature were the deep greens and blues — glass was used for these. Until recently, many scholars believed that glass mosaics came into use only in Byzantine times, but the excavations at Antioch have shown that they were already in use during the Roman period.

Pavements were laid according to one of two methods. The Roman method was to prepare a surrounding field with mainly geometric patterns and then to insert the mosaic pictures (emblemata) into this background. The *emblemata* were prepared separately in special workshops. This is the manner in which the fine mosaics of Pompeii and Antioch, which reproduce paintings, have come down to us. In the Byzantine period, as we have seen, the pavements were laid as a whole. Aesthetically, this was a more satisfactory procedure. First, the rough outline of the drawing was made on the top surface of the fine cement layer. Usually, the amount of space which could be covered in one day was drawn at one time. The master artist then filled in the figures and left two rows of white cubes surrounding them. The rest of the pavement, usually a simple white background, was completed by his apprentices.

There was an enormous amount of work involved in such mosaic pavements. It has been calculated that the mosaic map found at Medeba contains one and a half million mosaic cubes! Several workmen laboured for a year and a half to complete it. As we know, earlier mosaics were made of pebbles, while later on square pieces were cut from prepared stone plates. It was the Romans who distinguished the square cube mosaics from works in which pebbles of irregular size were used. Square cube mosaics were called *opus tesselatum* — the mosaic proper. Irregular stone work, where marble or stone was used to obtain finer shapes, was known as *opus vermiculatum*, from the Latin word *vermis,* "worm" — because of the wiggly shapes of the stones. The latter was also called *opus alexandrinum,* since it first came from Alexandria, capital of Egypt, where this style was mainly practised.

In a fine mosaic, the size of the cubes, and occasionally also their shape, varies. Especially fine cubes were used for delineating the faces, while backgrounds were formed of rougher and larger cubes. A high quality mosaic pavement usually contained more than one hundred cubes to a square decimetre.

In wall mosaics, the work was even more complicated and the number of cubes much greater. In the Church of St George in Saloniki, Greece, each cube is but a half-millimetre wide. It is estimated that forty thousand cubes were used to cover a square metre. In the dome of this church alone, 36 million cubes were used. Another example is the mausoleum of Empress Galla Placida at Ravenna, where some of the cubes are only three millimetres square.

In wall mosaics, which are more delicate than pavements, greater use was made of glass cubes, wherein many kinds of colours and shades could be obtained by mixing various metal oxides with the glass. Special treatment was necessary for the gold cubes which formed the main background of By-zantine wall mosaics. A thin gold foil was placed on top of a glass cube and covered with a thin plate of glass. By using such cubes with the glass plate on top and the gold beneath, the otherwise monotonous effect of the surface could be varied. The same result was achieved by the occasional use of pure glass cubes without the gold leaf. One technical trick which has been noticed in many wall mosaics was the use of cubes placed at an angle to the vertical line of the wall. As a result, the reflection of light upon the mosaic was refracted in various directions. This was an important factor in the aesthetic impact of the wall mosaics — the way in which the light rays were reflected added greatly to the general aesthetic effect.

The visual impact of wall mosaics was based on an impressionistic principle. The colours which strike the ends of the optic nerves are the result of a grouping of many small spots of various colours. Each produces a single ray of unbroken colour and these blend together to give the same result received from impres-sionist paintings, especially those of the tachist school. As we discussed pre-viously, this very lively effect was well understood in the Byzantine period and has been used with great effect in the various wall mosaics of that time.

Mosaic artists of the finest periods understood very well the art of creating an effective contrast. They knew that the pictures would be observed from a distance and that similar colours would blend together and would not bring out the contours of the images. For this reason, a series of colour contrasts was used in which many of the discoveries of the impressionist school were antic-ipated. A blue mountain, for instance, had an addition of purple shading. A red dress was coloured blue or dark green in its shaded folds. In some of the later mosaic works, for instance those found on the Aegean island of Chios, the folds were executed in gold while the dress was black.

2. *Preservation*

One advantage of mosaic art is that it is practically indestructible, at least as far as the cubes are concerned. Mosaic pavements, in particular, aston-ish us by the solidity of their work. Even when they were laid over vaults, people could still walk on them. Because the cubes are of the same material throughout their depth, their colour is still the same even though their surfaces may be worn down. On the other hand, pavements wore out quickly in places where many people walked on them, and as a result they had to be replaced quite often. Wall mosaics were as solid as the floor mosaics, although because their bases were walls, they were much more adversely affected by various natural or man-made disasters.

These mosaic works, whether on pavements or on walls, have provided us with some of antiquity's finest works of art. However, they present a great problem of preservation. In order to preserve wall mosaics from the start, a building must merely have its walls intact, and this does not present such a major problem. Also, parts of wall mosaics can even be transferred to museum walls without loss of aesthetic value. But to maintain mosaic pavements, the whole building must be reconstructed. An alternative method is to transfer parts of the pavements to museums. Otherwise, the display of the pavement would require as much floor space as the original building took up, and there are very few museums which can provide such an area.

In the museums themselves, the pavements must be cleaned constantly. This too, endangers their survival. In some cases, pavements have been kept under water to keep their colours fresh. In others, they have been oiled or treated with a special preparation. In many museums, such as the very fine Antioch Mosaic Museum, the pavements are displayed on walls. But this is an unsatisfactory compromise because the pavements were intended to be seen by the viewer as he looks down from above. When the mosaics are hung on a wall, they lose their special artistic impact.

Mosaic art is only one highly specialized medium of ancient art. But it is instructive both for the evolution of art in antiquity as a whole and even for the social developments of general character in ancient society, especially in its religious aspect. Mosaics are, in addition, visual artefacts of beauty and charm.

ILLUSTRATION SOURCES

Fratelli Alinari, Firenze, P. 15; 17–25; 66–69; 81–83. London University Press, P. 31. Israel Department of Antiquities and Museums, P. 37–40; 45; 46; 49; 50; 52; 54; 55; 57; 58; 60; 73; 76. Mansell Collection, London, P. 63. Albert Skira, Geneva, P. 71; 74; 75; 79; 80.

INDEX